CIVILIZATIONS OF THE ANCIENT WORLD

THE ANCIENT
MAYA

A MyReportLinks.com Book

SUZANNE LIEURANCE

MyReportLinks.com Books

an imprint of

 Enslow Publishers, Inc.

Box 398, 40 Industrial Road
Berkeley Heights, NJ 07922
USA

MyReportLinks.com Books, an imprint of Enslow Publishers, Inc. MyReportLinks®
is a registered trademark of Enslow Publishers, Inc.

Library of Congress Cataloging-in-Publication Data

Lieurance, Suzanne.
  The ancient Maya / Suzanne Lieurance.
     p. cm. — (Civilizations of the ancient world)
  Includes bibliographical references and index.
  ISBN 0-7660-5197-8
  1. Mayas—History. 2. Mayas—Social life and customs. I. Title. II. Series.
  F1435.L77 2004
  972.81—dc22
                                    2004000400

Printed in the United States of America

10 9 8 7 6 5 4 3 2 1

To Our Readers:
Through the purchase of this book, you and your library gain access to the Report Links that specifically back up this book.
The Publisher will provide access to the Report Links that back up this book and will keep these Report Links up to date on **www.myreportlinks.com** for three years from the book's first publication date.
We have done our best to make sure all Internet addresses in this book were active and appropriate when we went to press. However, the author and the Publisher have no control over, and assume no liability for, the material available on those Internet sites or on other Web sites they may link to.
The usage of the MyReportLinks.com Books Web site is subject to the terms and conditions stated on the Usage Policy Statement on **www.myreportlinks.com**.
A password may be required to access the Report Links that back up this book. The password is found on the bottom of page 4 of this book.
Any comments or suggestions can be sent by e-mail to comments@myreportlinks.com or to the address on the back cover.

Photo Credits: © Corel Corporation, pp. 1, 3, 11, 13, 14, 16, 23, 29, 30, 33, 36, 37, 40, 45; Ancient Mexico.com, p. 26; Canadian Museum of Civilization, pp. 21, 27, 32, 44; Clipart.com, p. 9; Enslow Publishers, Inc., p. 18; Florida State University, p. 24; MyReportLinks.com Books, pp. 4, back cover; Mariners' Museum, p. 42; PBS, p. 38; Science Museum of Minnesota, p. 19.

Cover Photo: Stone head, Copán; hillside temple, Palenque; and slate carving, © Corel Corporation.

Tools

Search

Notes

Discuss

MyReportLinks.com Books

Go!

Contents

THE ANCIENT MAYA

MyReportLinks.com Books
Great Books, Great Links, Great for Research!

The Report Links listed on the following four pages can save you hours of research time by **instantly** bringing you to the best Web sites relating to your report topic.

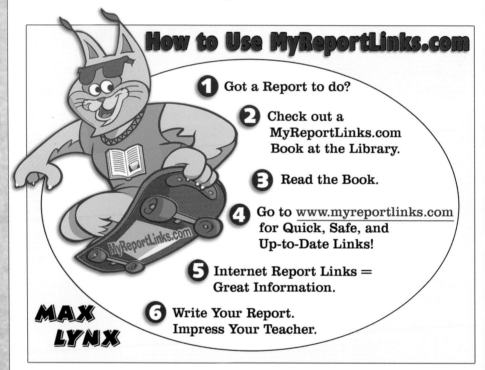

How to Use MyReportLinks.com

1. Got a Report to do?
2. Check out a MyReportLinks.com Book at the Library.
3. Read the Book.
4. Go to www.myreportlinks.com for Quick, Safe, and Up-to-Date Links!
5. Internet Report Links = Great Information.
6. Write Your Report. Impress Your Teacher.

MAX LYNX

The pre-evaluated Web sites are your links to source documents, photographs, illustrations, and maps. They also provide links to dozens—even hundreds—of Web sites about your report subject.

MyReportLinks.com Books and the MyReportLinks.com Web site save you time and make report writing easier than ever!

Please see "To Our Readers" on the copyright page for important information about this book, the MyReportLinks.com Web site, and the Report Links that back up this book. Please enter **VMA2997** if asked for a password.

Report Links

 The Internet sites described below can be accessed at http://www.myreportlinks.com

*EDITOR'S CHOICE

▶**The Maya Ruins Page**
The ancient Maya developed several sprawling city-states, including Tikal, Palenque, and Chichén Itzá, renowned for their amazing temples. This site offers a look at some of the major Maya cities as well as pictures of the ruins that remain.

*EDITOR'S CHOICE

▶**Mystery of the Maya**
At this Web site you can learn about Maya society, religious beliefs, art, architecture, and more.

*EDITOR'S CHOICE

▶**AncientMexico.com**
The Maya occupied a large portion of what is today the country of Mexico. Here you can learn about the people who lived in ancient Mexico, maps of where they lived, their religious beliefs, and much more.

*EDITOR'S CHOICE

▶**The Maya Region**
The ancient Maya lived in the region that today includes Mexico, Guatemala, Honduras, Belize, and El Salvador. This site offers a look at the land where the Maya lived and how the civilization was dispersed throughout the area.

*EDITOR'S CHOICE

▶**Mundo Maya Online**
This online newsletter presents articles on Maya culture, archaeological findings, daily life, art, and more.

*EDITOR'S CHOICE

▶**Calendars Through the Ages:
The Mayan Calendar**
One of the main accomplishments of the Maya was their complex calendar, which is somewhat similar to the one we use today. This site explains how the Maya calendar came about as well as how it works.

Report Links

The Internet sites described below can be accessed at http://www.myreportlinks.com

▶**Cacao—Science Museum of Minnesota**

The ancient Maya were one of the first groups of people to grow cacao, a bean used to make chocolate. Here you can learn about the origins of chocolate, how it is grown, and how it was used in the Maya civilization.

▶**Cities of the Ancient Maya**

This Web site contains all sorts of information on the ancient Maya, including sections on the major cities, archaeological discoveries, Maya books and codices, and the Spanish conquest of Mesoamerica.

▶**Collapse: Why Do Civilizations Fall?**

One aspect of the Maya that remains a mystery is how and why it disappeared. At this interactive Web site, you can learn about the collapse of the ancient Maya, as well as other civilizations, and take part in activities that may offer clues to what led to their collapse.

▶**Droughts Ended Maya Civilization, Experts Say**

While the exact reasons for the Maya civilization's downfall remain a mystery, some think it could have had to do with climate and drought. This *National Geographic* article explains how droughts may have played a part in the Maya's collapse.

▶**The Explorations of Christopher Columbus**

Christopher Columbus's first voyage in 1492 to the lands of the Western Hemisphere paved the way for European exploration and settlement. This site offers a brief account of his explorations.

▶**How Did the Average Maya Live?**

While the ancient Maya cities are known for their temples, the average Maya houses were quite different from the stone structures that made the cities famous. Take a look at some average Maya homes and buildings at this site.

▶**John L. Stephens**

Explorer John L. Stephens was one of the first Americans to explore the ancient cities of the Maya. Learn about his life and travels at this site.

▶**The Living Maya**

Though the ancient Maya civilization ended nearly one thousand years ago, Mesoamerica is still home to many Maya descendants. Find out about the history of their culture, their old and new beliefs, their language, and more.

The Internet sites described below can be accessed at
http://www.myreportlinks.com

▶**Lords of Copán**

On this PBS site, you can read about an archaeological expedition in Copán
and what Mayan artifacts were found there.

▶**Lost King of the Maya**

This Web site from PBS explores findings in the city of Copán, near the
Honduras-Guatemala border. Learn about the Maya artifacts found here
along with information on other cities of the Maya civilization.

▶**Maya Adventure**

At this interactive Web site, you can take a virtual tour of the areas where
the ancient Maya lived. Photographs and activities are included.

▶**The Maya Astronomy Page**

The Maya are known for their significant contributions to the worlds of math
and science. On this site learn about the Maya's impact on astronomy, math,
writing, language, and more.

▶**Maya Hieroglyphs Recount "Giant War"**

It is believed that the ancient Maya city-states fought with one another in order
to gain power. In this article, you can read about how an ancient hieroglyphic
inscription might offer clues to the relationships between the Maya cities.

▶**Maya Stories**

Ancient Maya culture produced many interesting stories and folktales.
You can read some of these stories by following the links provided on
this Web site.

▶**Maya Weaving Traditions**

The Maya produced traditional garments by weaving—and still do. Learn about
the tradition of Maya weaving and view images of traditional clothing here.

▶**A Mayan Game of Chance**

The ancient Maya played a game of chance known as *bul*. At this Web site, you
can learn the rules to bul, and once you are familiar with the rules, you can play
the game.

Report Links

The Internet sites described below can be accessed at http://www.myreportlinks.com

▶Mayan Gods, Mythology

The ancient Maya had very strong and unique religious beliefs. Here you can find out about their different gods and goddesses and how those deities influenced the lives of the Maya people.

▶Mayan Kids

At this Web site, made specifically for kids, you can find out a lot about Maya culture and history—from Maya people and places to their unique religious and spiritual beliefs.

▶Mesoamerican Art

The art and architecture of the ancient Maya are renowned for their uniqueness and beauty. Take a look at some of the Maya's most noteworthy pieces and places at this Web site.

▶Palenque

This site offers photographs of many of the ruins of the great Maya city-state of Palenque, in south-central Mexico. Click on the images to see larger views of the ruins, including the Temple of the Sun and Pakal's glyph.

▶Rigoberta Menchú Tum—Biography

Rigoberta Menchú Tum is a Maya woman who was awarded the Nobel Peace Prize in 1992. Read about her life and contributions to the modern Maya at this site, which contains links to her acceptance speech, Nobel lecture, and more.

▶ScienceDaily News Release

In November 2003, archaeologists recovered an ancient Maya stone altar from the year A.D. 796. This site examines the restoration of this ancient ruin and what it can tell people today about the Maya kingdom.

▶Tour of Chichén Itzá

Chichén Itzá was one of the ancient Maya's most celebrated cities. At this site, you can learn about this historic place and view vivid pictures of the city's architectural monuments.

▶Writing

The ancient Maya developed a complex system of writing made up of hieroglyphic symbols. At this Web site, you can find out about the history of Maya writing and how it is interpreted.

Time Line

c.2500 B.C.	**Archaic Period** The beginnings of Maya civilization in Mesoamerica.
c.2000 B.C.	The Olmec civilization, which influences Maya culture, develops.
c.1800 B.C.–A.D. 250	**Preclassic Period**
1800–1000 B.C.	*Early Preclassic Period* Maya probably lived near sources of water, hunted and fished, and gathered wild plants for food.
1000–300 B.C.	*Middle Preclassic Period* First evidence of Maya villages and some evidence of large-scale architecture; earliest solar calendars developed.
300 B.C.–A.D. 250	*Late Preclassic Period* Hierarchical society begins, including rule by kings; spread of cities and monumental architecture.
c.A.D. 250–900	**Classic Period** The peak of Maya civilization in which the great city-states thrive and art and architecture flourish.
A.D. 900–1530	**Postclassic Period** The great city-state of Tikal declines, and other southern lowland cities collapse. Maya cities in northern Yucatán continue to thrive, however.
1517	Spanish arrive on shores of Yucatán, and within a century, diseases and enslavement kill nearly all native population in Mesoamerica.
1528	Spanish begin their conquest of the Maya, although several Maya groups continue fighting for the rest of the century.

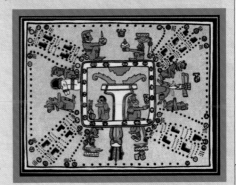

A Maya calendar.

Chapter 1 ▶

THE MYSTERY OF THE ANCIENT MAYA

More than a thousand years before the first Europeans arrived in the Western Hemisphere, an extraordinary American Indian people known as the Maya had created one of the most advanced civilizations in the world. The ancient Maya built great cities where thousands of people lived, yet they had no metal tools and no pack animals for transporting the huge stones they used as building materials. They were among the first civilizations in the Western Hemisphere to develop a writing system, and they were early mathematicians and astronomers whose accurate calculations led to a calendar based on the earth's orbit around the sun.

By about A.D. 900, the Maya had abandoned their elaborate cities in the lowlands of what is today Guatemala. Some cities were deserted even before they were completed. Why the Maya left their great cities has remained a mystery for centuries.

▶ The Crowning Glory of the Maya

The ancient Maya civilization lasted nearly four thousand years, from about 2500 B.C. to A.D. 1528, but reached its peak from about A.D. 250 to 900. During this Classic Period of Maya civilization the ancient Maya created an advanced calendar, built massive tombs for their dead kings, and made elaborate carvings on freestanding stone slabs called *stelae*, which recorded important historical events.

The Maya recorded the important events of their history on stone monuments known as stelae, like this one at Yasheelan.

Great Cities of the Maya

For several centuries, many large Maya cities rose and fell in areas from the northern plains of the Yucatán Peninsula in what is today Mexico to the tropical jungle of Petén in what is currently Guatemala. Archaeologists, scientists who study people of the past and their cultures through the materials they leave behind, have uncovered information about the ancient Maya from excavating lost Maya cities such as Palenque, Tikal, Uxmal, Copán, and Chichén Itzá.

Tikal

Tikal was a large and wealthy Maya city in the dense lowland jungle of Petén, in present-day northern Guatemala. At one point, Tikal's population might have reached more than fifty thousand, including those who lived in rural areas outside the city.

Tikal was located on one of the few passable overland routes between two rivers. Traders traveling between these two rivers had to pass through Tikal, and the city became wealthy from the money it charged these traders to use their city as a thoroughfare.

The center of Tikal was crowded with palaces and temples built on top of tall pyramids that featured flat tops. Some of these pyramids are the highest known structures built in the ancient Americas. The outer walls of these palaces and pyramids contained symbolic figures and characters known as glyphs that were carved into the stone and often painted a brilliant shade of red. To the ancient Maya, red was an important color because it signified blood and life. Red pigment was easily made from a common mineral known as hematite.

Palenque

Palenque was a large city that flourished from A.D. 431 to about 810, during the height of ancient Maya civilization. It may have been home to as many as ten thousand people. It did not take long for the jungle to grow up around Palenque after it was abandoned, so the once-great city virtually disappeared until 1786, when a Spanish army captain named Antonio del Rio rediscovered it. He and his men spent many days clearing the jungle to reveal what was left of the magnificent buildings that had been constructed there so long ago.

After del Rio's visit, Palenque was largely forgotten again until 1831, when an adventurer named Jean Frederic Maximilien de Waldeck traveled to the ruins. De Waldeck decided to live at Palenque for two years to make drawings of the city. A few years later, an American explorer named John Lloyd Stephens, along with a British

▲ *The ruins of the palace at Palenque, one of the great Maya city-states.*

artist named Frederick Catherwood, traveled to Palenque to explore the site and record what they saw. Stephens discovered that the Maya had built an elaborate aqueduct system there, which had once supplied Palenque with drinking water.

Archaeologists have studied Palenque for more than a hundred years. In 1952, they discovered the elaborate tomb of King Pakal by following a stairway that led from the floor of a temple to the base of a pyramid. They also found a four-story square tower in Palenque's main palace complex, which they think might have functioned as an observatory. But excavation in the jungle is a slow and tedious process, and there are still many buildings at Palenque as yet unexplored.

Uxmal

Just as the Maya were deserting their cities in the central and southern lowlands, a great city known as Uxmal was taking shape farther north, in the Yucatán Peninsula of Mexico. The city of Uxmal, perhaps the most elegant of the ancient Maya cities, was quite different from Palenque and Tikal. Its structures featured an architectural style known as Puuc in which building facades were decorated with elaborate mosaics. Some of those mosaics were large masks of the rain god, Chaac.

The Palace of the Governor in Uxmal is a graceful structure. In 1840, when John Lloyd Stephens saw it, he compared it to other examples of great architecture around the world, commenting that "if it stood . . . in Hyde Park or the Garden of the Tuileries, it would form a new order . . . not unworthy to stand beside the remains of Egyptian, Greek and Roman art."[1] Uxmal flourished for many years, but by the time of the Spanish conquest in the 1500s, it had also been abandoned.

▲ The pyramid at Uxmal in the Yucatán Peninsula shows that while some Maya cities were on the decline, those in the north were flourishing.

Chichén Itzá

Chichén Itzá, a Maya city on the Yucatán Peninsula, flourished from the seventh through the early thirteenth centuries A.D., long after the great Maya cities of the south had been abandoned. One of the more fascinating structures created at any time by the Maya can be found at Chichén Itzá. It is called the Temple of Kukulcán. Every year, at about 3:00 in the afternoon, on the first days of spring and fall (the equinoxes), something astonishing takes place at this pyramid. The sun creates a shadow on its stairs and also at its base that appears to be a snake slithering down the stairs to the ground. To the ancient Maya, this shadow represented the body of Kukulcán, the feathered serpent god of the wind and learning.

Solving the Mysteries

Archaeologists have yet to find out why the great Maya civilization started to decline and why many of its magnificent cities were simply abandoned around A.D. 900. But in the last fifty years, archaeologists and historians have learned more about what the ancient Maya were like.

At first, archaeologists thought the Maya had been a gentle people who spent their days peacefully worshipping their gods and planting their crops, without engaging in wars with one another or exhibiting violent behavior in other ways. But as more Maya ruins and artifacts were uncovered, excavated, and studied, a much different picture of the ancient Maya was revealed. Scientists learned that the ancient Maya did grow crops, and they did worship their gods. But they were also a fierce people who fought wars against each other for control of the largest Maya cities, known as city-states. In addition to

▲ An ornately carved rattlesnake is featured on the walls of a Maya building in Uxmal.

the blood that was shed on the field of battle, the ancient Maya also shed their own blood and the blood of animals as a sacrifice to their gods so that their crops would not fail and the gods would be happy with them.

As to why the great Maya civilization disappeared, archaeologists and historians have formed certain opinions. Some believe that, as Maya cities grew, it became more difficult to feed everyone because there simply was not enough fertile land left near the cities to raise enough food. Others point to a catastrophic climate change they believe affected the civilization's downfall. Gerald Haug, a professor of geology at the University of Potsdam, in Germany, believes a severe and prolonged drought led to the Maya's demise.[2] Archaeologists continue working to uncover the mysteries of the ancient Maya.

Chapter 2 ▶

THE LAND OF THE ANCIENT MAYA

The Maya lived in Mesoamerica, the southern part of North America that was home to civilizations before the arrival of Columbus in 1492. Their lands spread for nearly 120,000 square miles in what is today southern Mexico, Guatemala, Belize, Honduras, and El Salvador.

They lived in three geographical zones in these areas—the lowlands, the highlands, and the Pacific coastal plain. The geography of these areas determined how the Maya in each place lived. The earliest Maya civilizations were thought to have settled along the coast. During the height of Maya civilization, many of the great cities developed in the rain forests of the Guatemalan lowlands. It was not until after the end of this period that the Maya left the lowlands and moved north, settling in the Yucatán Peninsula and south, to the highlands of southern Guatemala.

The Lowlands

The Maya settled in both the southern lowlands and the northern lowlands of Mesoamerica. The northern lowlands were hot and dry, and even in the rainy season, from May through October, there was little rainfall. This area also lacks natural rivers and lakes, so the Maya had to find water in *cenotes*, deep natural wells made of soft limestone.

The southern lowlands region, made up of rain forests and savannas (grassland with scattered trees), receives more rain than the northern areas and is also home to many lakes,

rivers, and swamps, so surface water was more plentiful for the Maya living there.

▶ The Highlands

The highlands are made up of the mountains and valleys of the Sierra Madre, which consists of three major mountain chains in Mexico. Over the years, ash from erupting volcanoes made the soil very rich in the highlands, making it an excellent place for growing food. The climate in the highlands is also cooler than it is in the lowlands.

▲ This map shows the lands of the Maya in Mesoamerica. Maya cities and settlements spread from Mexico to El Salvador.

Chocolate - Science Museum of Minnesota - Microsoft Internet Explorer

File Edit View Favorites Tools Help

Address 🗐 http://www.sci.mus.mn.us/sln/tf/c/chocolate/chocolate.html   🖉 Go

Chocolate

Glyphs on this vessel
tell a story
that dates to the year
754.

Q. **What does this have to do with chocolate?**

The ancient Maya drank chocolate drinks out of vessels
like this one found at Altar de Sacrificios, Guatemala.

Q. **Where did the Maya get chocolate?**

The Maya cultivated or grew a type of tree (Theobroma
Cacao) that produces cacao pods that are filled with
cocoa beans. The beans were crushed into a powder then
mixed into a ceremonial drink.

Internet

▲ *An ancient Maya vessel used for chocolate drinks.*

The rainy season is between May and November, with
the heaviest rainfall coming in June and October.

▶ The Pacific Coastal Plain

The earliest Maya lived along the Pacific coast, which features a tropical climate. The ancient Maya who lived here
fished, hunted, and also grew cacao trees that produce a
type of bean that was ground into cocoa powder and used
to make a chocolate drink. Cacao beans were very pre-
cious to the Maya and were sometimes exchanged when
the Maya bartered.

Chapter 3

THE CULTURE OF THE ANCIENT MAYA

Ancient Maya society was made up of several classes: the elite, the common people, and the slaves. The elite class was divided into subclasses. First came the royalty, made up of the rulers and noblemen; next were the priests, then the craftspeople, and finally the wealthy merchants. The common people were farmers who also hunted, fished, and served as soldiers and laborers. Slaves made up the lowest class in Maya society. Many slaves had been captured during war.

▶ Maya Families

As with most cultures, the family was very important to the ancient Maya. Men and women usually married between the ages of sixteen and twenty. Their marriages were often arranged by a matchmaker. After marriage, couples lived with the husband's parents for at least a while.

Families (the mother, the father, and their children) lived together in a single house. Their extended family groups lived nearby. All the homes were clustered together, which made it easier for families to work together.

Men produced the food for their families. Most early Maya were farmers who lived and worked together in small villages. They cleared fields and dug ditches by using tools made of stone. They made holes in the ground with pointed sticks so that they could plant seeds. Eventually they developed more advanced farming techniques. They learned how to rotate crops and fertilize

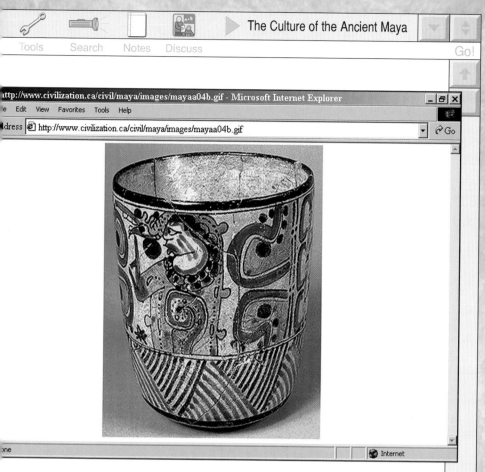

http://www.civilization.ca/civil/maya/images/mayaa04b.gif - Microsoft Internet Explorer

File   Edit   View   Favorites   Tools   Help

Address http://www.civilization.ca/civil/maya/images/mayaa04b.gif

▲ *This painted terra-cotta vessel dates from the Classic Period of Maya civilization. It features two dancing figures who represent the gods of death, with a snake rising up their backs.*

them. They also developed a system of terraced farming on hillsides and they drained swamps, which increased the amount of land that could be used to grow crops. Men also hunted and fished to provide their families with food.

Women in Maya culture had many jobs. They prepared and cooked the food for the entire family. They also gathered firewood and fetched water from wells and wove cotton into cloth for the family's clothing. Children helped out with the daily chores as soon as they were about five or six years old. Younger children played most of the time.

Education

Boys from noble families went to school when they were about fifteen years old to study reading, writing, math, astronomy, and religion. But the Maya children of the common class did not go to school, so they probably never learned to read. Instead, their parents taught them how to farm, make cloth, and help out in other ways with the work at home.

Food, Clothing, and Shelter

The staple food of the Maya was corn, which they grew along with beans, squash, mango, papaya, cassava, and avocado. They also ate the meat of animals they hunted and fish caught in the ocean, rivers, and lakes.

A favorite meal for the Maya was stew. Maya women used a variety of ingredients to make different kinds of stew. Corn kernels ground into a thick paste would thicken the liquid of the stew. A long cylindrical stone called a *mano* was used to grind corn on a flat stone called a *metate*. Ground corn was an important part of the Maya diet; it was used to make a variety of foods including tortillas, tamales, corn loaves, and even corn porridge.

The Maya made an interesting drink by crushing chili peppers and then combining them with chocolate powder they made from ground cacao beans. This powder was then mixed with water in a cup or pot, making a chocolate drink that was probably rather spicy. The Maya poured this liquid from one container to another, over and over again, until it became foamy or frothy.

The clothing for most Maya was very simple and usually made of cotton. Generally, people from the upper class wore colorful clothing, often decorated with designs

▲ The ancient Maya city of Copán features extraordinary sculptures, like this face carved from stone.

Huipil - Microsoft Internet Explorer

File   Edit   View   Favorites   Tools   Help

Address   http://www.anthro.fsu.edu/wovenvoices/weaving/huipil.html

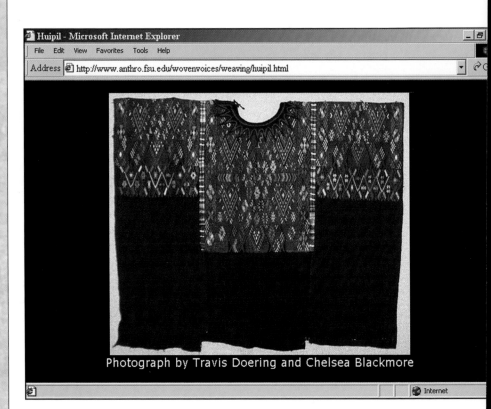

Photograph by Travis Doering and Chelsea Blackmore

Internet

▲ *Maya women still wear huipils, like the one shown above. This traditional blouse identifies the village of the wearer as well as her social and marital status and her religious beliefs.*

and feathers. The clothing of the lower class featured little color and no decoration.

Men usually wore loincloths, strips of cloth wrapped around the waist, pulled up between the legs, and tied in front. They did not usually wear shirts, probably because the weather was quite warm. Women wore skirts and loose embroidered blouses called huipils. Women with babies often wore a mantle, which was a long piece of cloth draped over the woman's head and used as a sling for carrying the baby.

Maya homes were usually built of sun-dried mud or bricks called *adobe* or mud smeared over a framework of wooden poles. The walls and floors of these houses were often covered with plaster. The houses of common people were generally built on low mounds of earth, while the homes of the nobility were built on higher platforms made of stone. There were no windows and only one door in a Maya house. The roof was made of dried grass and sloped so that rain would run off of it easily. The only furnishings in an ancient Maya home were jars and baskets used to store things and some reed mats that were used as chairs and beds.

Because the Maya believed that their ancestors watched over them, they buried their dead relatives beneath their houses.

▶ Religion

Religion was an important part of life for the ancient Maya, who believed in many gods and goddesses, including a creator god, Hunab Ku; a rain god, Chaac; a sun god, Kinich Ahau; and a moon goddess and the goddess of weaving, medicine, and childbirth, Ix Chel.

Like other people of their time, the Maya believed that the earth was flat. Unlike other cultures, however, the Maya envisioned the earth on the back of a crocodile that floated in a large pond. They also believed that there were thirteen layers of heaven above earth and nine underworlds below it.

In Maya belief, the world had gone through four creations and they were living during the fifth creation. The first four worlds had been destroyed by various disasters. The Maya also believed that the gods had created human

beings from corn, so that plant did more than nourish and sustain them—they were spiritually linked to it.

Many of the Maya's religious ceremonies began with prayers, gifts, and sacrificial offerings to the gods. Blood was a regular offering to the gods. Sometimes the blood of animals was offered, but human blood from people captured during war was also given to the gods. Men and women would also pierce themselves to draw blood and offer it as a sacrifice.

Another way in which the Maya would offer a human sacrifice to their gods was to throw the victim or victims into a sacred well. If the victim survived the fall and did

The Gods of Mexico and the Maya - Microsoft Internet Explorer

File   Edit   View   Favorites   Tools   Help

Address http://www.ancientmexico.com/content/gods/kinichahau.html

Moon Goddess
Water Lily Jaguar
Rabbit Scribe
Jaguar Baby
Chac
Kinich Ahau
Bolon Dzacab
Chac-Xib-Chac

KINICH AHAU
THE SUN GOD

Kinich Ahau, which means the sun eyed lord, was the god of the sun.
He was associated with the jaguar, the most powerful denizen of the Mayan forests.
He was shown as a young man, full of life and vigour like the rising sun itself.

Done   Internet

▲ There were many gods and goddesses in the Maya religion. This illustration shows the sun god, Kinich Ahau, who was associated with the jaguar—also an important creature to the Maya.

not drown, the priests pulled him or her out of the well, believing that the gods had decided to spare this person and had spoken to him or her. The priests then asked the victim what message had been received from the gods. The victim was then spared and given special treatment for the rest of his or her life.

Blood Sport

Even the sports that the ancient Maya participated in had religious significance. The Maya felt that their entire way of life depended on the outcome of a ball game called pok-a-tok. Pok-a-tok courts, which were in the shape of a capital

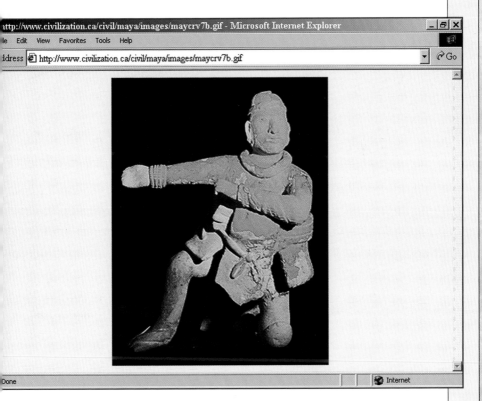

http://www.civilization.ca/civil/maya/images/maycrv7b.gif - Microsoft Internet Explorer

File   Edit   View   Favorites   Tools   Help

Address http://www.civilization.ca/civil/maya/images/maycrv7b.gif   Go

Done   Internet

This figure is of a Maya ballplayer, who symbolizes the life-and-death battle that took place during the third creation.

letter I and flanked on each side by slanted stone walls, could be found in many Maya villages. The ball represented the sun and moon, and the ball court represented the earth. Some archaeologists believe the game might have served as a substitute for war. But, whether or not that is true, losers still paid the ultimate price: Members of the losing team were sometimes sacrificed to please the gods.

The object of the game was to move the large, heavy ball from one side of the court to the other and get it into the open end of the other team's side of the court, but the players could not use their hands or feet to keep the ball in play. Instead, they used other parts of their body—mainly their waists or chests, which were wrapped with protective "yokes." These yokes kept the heavy ball from crushing a player's ribs as he hit the ball.

The largest ancient ball court in Mesoamerica is found at Chichén Itzá. It includes reliefs, or raised carvings, depicting the human sacrifices that were carried out as part of the ball game.

▶ The Maya Ideal of Beauty

The Maya ideal of beauty was one that most people would find strange today. It stemmed from their belief that all humankind had been created from an ear of corn. Pictures of their corn god show him with an elongated head with a husk attached to it. When a baby was born to the nobility, the baby's head was bound between two boards for several days to reshape the skull, leaving it elongated and flat, like an ear of corn—to the Maya, a sign of true beauty.[1]

The Maya also thought it was attractive to be cross-eyed, so they would hang a ball or bright bead on a strand of thread close to a baby's face. As the baby stared at it, his eyes would become crossed.

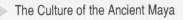

▲ This carving of a Maya with a bound head can be found at the ruins of Palenque.

Sharp teeth were also favored by the Maya, so they would file their teeth into sharp points and then fill in the gaps between the teeth with colorful materials such as pyrite, a yellowish mineral; obsidian, a dark natural glass formed from volcanic ash; or jade, a green gemstone. The Maya also tattooed themselves and painted their bodies bright colors in an effort to be beautiful.

Chapter 4

AMAZING ACHIEVEMENTS OF THE MAYA

The ancient Maya produced some of the most fascinating architecture and writing of the ancient Americas, and their advancements in mathematics and astronomy were well ahead of their time. The Maya were one of the first civilizations to understand and use the concept of zero. Their counting system used only three symbols: A dot or circle represented a value of one, a straight bar represented five, and an oval figure represented zero. Even uneducated people could do simple calculations and conduct trade with these three symbols.

▲ This ancient Maya calendar is from Cancún, in what is now Mexico. The Maya's expertise in mathematics and astronomy led them to create calendars that were remarkably accurate.

The ancient Maya developed calendars to determine when to hold religious ceremonies, have feasts, conduct wars, and determine the right times for other important events. The Maya combined their knowledge of mathematics and astronomy to create several highly accurate calendars. Their first calendar was the "sacred calendar." It was based on 260 days arranged in 20 months of 13 days each.

Their second calendar marked the "vague year." It had 365 days (based on the orbit of the earth around the sun) arranged in 18 months of 20 days each, with 5 days at the end of the year. These five extra days were thought to be very unlucky, so during them, the Maya fasted, made sacrifices to their gods, and did not work.

The Maya had a third calendar, which was called the "long count." It was used for about four hundred years and was arranged in differently named and numbered counts of 360 days each. The long count started with the beginning of the current creation cycle in their belief system, in the years 3113 or 3114 B.C. of our modern calendar.

Sculpture and Writing

The Maya developed a complex writing system that consisted of symbols, or glyphs, to record important events in their history. This ancient form of writing was carved into stone sculpture, appeared in books, and was painted on pottery. It has only been in recent years that epigraphers, scientists who are able to decipher symbolic writing such as hieroglyphics, have been able to decode some of the Maya glyphs and uncover a great deal more about their history.

Maya artists were called on to create stelae, stone monuments, to honor Maya royalty. The artists would carve information about Maya kings and other nobility into stelae using hieroglyphic texts. This was a way of

Back | Forward | Stop | Review | Home | Explore | Favorites | History

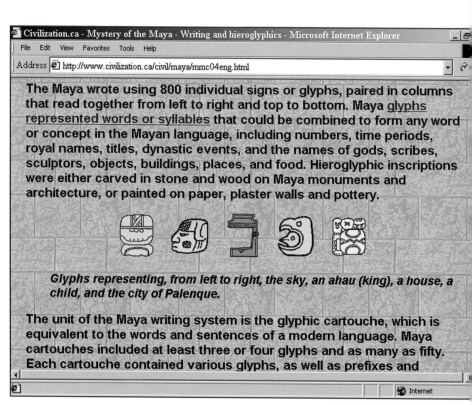

Civilization.ca - Mystery of the Maya - Writing and hieroglyphics - Microsoft Internet Explorer

File   Edit   View   Favorites   Tools   Help

Address http://www.civilization.ca/civil/maya/mmc04eng.html

The Maya wrote using 800 individual signs or glyphs, paired in columns that read together from left to right and top to bottom. Maya glyphs represented words or syllables that could be combined to form any word or concept in the Mayan language, including numbers, time periods, royal names, titles, dynastic events, and the names of gods, scribes, sculptors, objects, buildings, places, and food. Hieroglyphic inscriptions were either carved in stone and wood on Maya monuments and architecture, or painted on paper, plaster walls and pottery.

Glyphs representing, from left to right, the sky, an ahau (king), a house, a child, and the city of Palenque.

The unit of the Maya writing system is the glyphic cartouche, which is equivalent to the words and sentences of a modern language. Maya cartouches included at least three or four glyphs and as many as fifty. Each cartouche contained various glyphs, as well as prefixes and

Internet

▲ Glyphs were the written symbols of the Maya. They were carved into stelae and also written in books. Archaeologists are still trying to decipher the meanings of many Maya glyphs.

keeping a record of a king's reign. The king's birth date, information about his marriage, the date he became king, and important battles were all recorded on these monuments. Stelae stood in the plazas of each city-state, and some were more than thirty feet high.

Figures and motifs were also carved on buildings, staircases, roofs, columns, and doorways of temples. Life-size stone sculptures can still be found in ancient Maya ruins.

The Maya also made books whose paper came from tree bark coated with lime to bleach it white. The books, called codices, were then folded like an accordion and bound with wood and deer hide. Codices were probably used by priests or rulers to determine important seasonal dates.

When the Spanish arrived in the Maya lands by the 1500s, they destroyed most of the Maya codices because Spanish priests considered the books to contain writings that contradicted the teachings of the Roman Catholic Church. Only four codices have survived because they were saved and sent to Europe by Spanish soldiers.

► Maya Architecture: Temples and Pyramids

The huge stone pyramids built by the ancient Maya in the heart of their cities are amazing feats of construction, especially when one realizes that they had no metal tools and no wheeled vehicles to transport the heavy stone to their building sites. The only tools available to them that could turn limestone into blocks were made from a stone known as chert. Chert was flaked and made into axes and

▲ The Maya temple-pyramid is an amazing feat of architecture. This is the Temple of the Warriors, found at the great Maya city of Chichén Itzá.

other tools that the Maya could use to pierce, cut, and scrape. Obsidian, a volcanic glass with razor-sharp edges, was flaked and formed into blades that also made effective cutting tools.

The center of each pyramid was a core of rocks and dirt surrounded by a retaining wall. From the base, platforms were stacked one on top of the other. These platforms decreased in size as they went up the base, creating stairs. The stairs were so narrow that a person could only climb them by turning his feet sideways. Maya temples were built on top of these pyramids. They were places where Maya priests could communicate with the many Maya gods.

A pyramid's exterior was covered with a thick layer of stucco, which was smoothed and then painted red or another bright color. Royalty were buried in elaborate tombs in the lower platforms of these pyramids.

Pottery and Masks

Without having access to a potter's wheel or kiln, the ancient Maya created beautiful pottery, mostly molded ceramics and pots formed from coils of clay. The pottery created for Maya royalty was colorful and elaborately decorated and often bore a hieroglyphic inscription. The pottery used by the common people to hold or store things was much plainer.

The Maya were also known for their ceremonial masks, which were carved from jade, wood, stucco, or shells. Some of these masks were simple, but others were elaborate works of art. Ceremonial masks were made to look like animals and gods—or sometimes combinations of both. Death masks were made for the kings to wear when they died. The Maya believed that these masks protected their rulers from any harm that might come to them in the afterlife.

Chapter 5 ▶

THE ANCIENT MAYA GOVERNMENT

The ancient Maya believed that their kings were descended from the gods, which led to powerful dynasties that shaped their civilization. In recent years, archaeologists and other scientists have learned more about some of the great leaders from ancient Maya cities such as Tikal, Palenque, and Calakmul that has also revealed much about the politics, wars, and survival of the ancient Maya. There are still many unanswered questions, however, about the great dynasties and governments of the ancient Maya.

The ancient Maya civilization was not made up of just one area ruled by a single king. Instead, the Maya were spread out over many different land areas, with many different rulers. During the Classic period of Maya history (A.D. 250–900), the civilization was divided into more than sixty kingdoms.[1] But different Maya kingdoms shared many of the same beliefs, customs, and traits.

▶ City-States

The Maya empire was made up of city-states, which consisted of the largest cities and the lands and people that surrounded them. Each city-state featured a strong and centralized government governed by a ruling class.[2] Every city-state had a complex known as a great plaza, home to the most important temples and the king's palace. The largest Maya city-states also had several smaller plazas. In addition to the royal family and other nobles, skilled craftspeople lived in the cities so that they could make

pottery and jewelry for the kings, nobles, and priests. These plazas were the center of government activity and religious ceremonies during Maya times. According to archaeologist Robert J. Sharer, "A center's size, together with the elaborateness of its buildings, the quantity of its monuments and hieroglyphic inscriptions, and its other characteristics, undoubtedly reflected its relative political and economic power."[3]

Some city-states were more powerful than others, and there were wars between them. Different city-states became powerful at different times. When they were not fighting, city-states conducted trade with one another.

▶ The Ajaw: Lord and Ruler

Each Maya city-state had its own king, called the *ajaw* (pronounced ah-HAW), which means "lord and ruler." The

▲ *Tikal, whose ruins are pictured, was home to great Maya leaders.*

▲ *The Maya temple and great plaza at Tikal.*

ajaw and his family and other members of the nobility lived in the city along with their servants. In addition to being the head of government, the ajaw led religious ceremonies. He wore elaborate and colorful clothes and a very large headdress. Less powerful city-states were often protected by more powerful ones, and the ajaw of the less powerful city-state had to obey the ajaw of the more powerful city-state.

It was the job of each ajaw to lead his soldiers in battle when they fought against other city-states. City-states did not have standing armies, but warfare and tribute (payments made by a less powerful ruler to a more powerful one) were important to the ajaw. Wars were often waged to obtain tribute and captives for sacrifice.

The worst thing that could happen to an ajaw was to become the prisoner of another city-state and its ajaw. The captured ajaw would be publicly humiliated and often tortured before being sacrificed.

Chapter 6 ▶

THE HISTORY
OF THE
ANCIENT MAYA

The four-thousand-year history of the ancient Maya civilization can be divided into four main periods. Little is known about the archaic period. Most of what is known about the Maya comes from the three most recent periods: the Preclassic Period, the Classic Period, and the Postclassic Period.

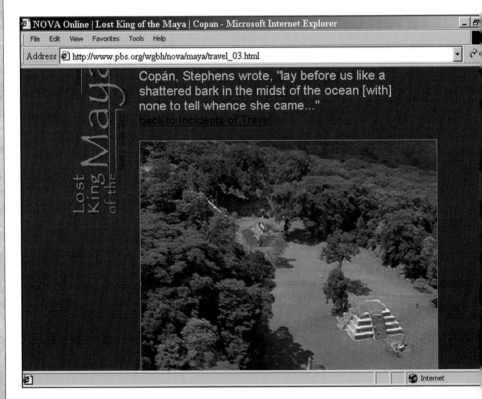

NOVA Online | Lost King of the Maya | Copan - Microsoft Internet Explorer

File　Edit　View　Favorites　Tools　Help

Address http://www.pbs.org/wgbh/nova/maya/travel_03.html

Copán, Stephens wrote, "lay before us like a shattered bark in the midst of the ocean [with] none to tell whence she came..."
back to Incidents of Travel

Internet

▲ A view of the ruins at Copán, in western Honduras. Scholars know that this once-great Maya city was abandoned early in the tenth century, but they do not know what brought about its decline.

The Preclassic Period

The Preclassic Period in Maya history lasted from about 1800 B.C. to A.D. 250. It can be divided further into the early, middle, and late Preclassic Periods.

The Early Preclassic Period, from 1800 B.C. to 1000 B.C., was a time before Maya cities were constructed. The Maya who lived during this period probably lived near the coast or swamps, lakes, and rivers. They probably hunted, fished, and gathered wild plants for food. They later began to grow corn. Maya homes of the period were made mainly of wooden poles and palm thatch.

The Middle Preclassic Period in Maya history lasted from about 1000 B.C. to 300 B.C. It was from this period that archaeologists have found the first evidence of settlements and villages that contained small wooden houses built on stone foundations. During the end of this period, villages started to move inland from the coast.

The late Preclassic Period lasted from about 300 B.C. to A.D. 250. It was a time of rapid population growth and the building of large cities. Large public structures, including palaces and temples, were built, and stone was used more extensively as a building material. Advances in farming, including the use of irrigation, began. Trade between cities increased greatly, and the rule by kings and an elite class became established.

The Classic Period

The Classic Period of Maya civilization lasted from about A.D. 250 to 900, the high point or "crowning glory" of the Maya. Kings and the elite were becoming a hereditary class, meaning that the sons of kings succeeded their fathers as rulers. The kings and elite used religion to direct

▲ *The reclining figure, typically found in Toltec and Maya temples, is known as a Chac-Mool, which in Mayan means "Red Jaguar."*

the daily life of the common people. The great pyramids and palaces of the Maya were built, repaired, and rebuilt during this time.

Art, science, religion, and writing flourished during the Classic Period. The end of this period is marked by a tremendous increase in political power struggles and war, perhaps due to conflicts over limited resources. These disputes and wars greatly reduced the population of some areas while other areas thrived.

The Postclassic Period

The Postclassic Period in Maya history lasted from about A.D. 900 to 1530. Overall, it was a time of great decline for the Maya civilization. However, some areas in the north continued to thrive during this period while population centers in the southern lowlands were completely abandoned.

Many coastal cities and trading centers were built and grew powerful during this era, even as the total civilization was declining. The large population centers broke into small warring factions. A few cities survived until the arrival of the Spanish around 1511 and the beginning of their conquest of the Yucatán in 1528.

The Spanish Conquest

After Christopher Columbus set foot in the Americas in 1492, he returned to Spain with tales of a land filled with riches. That news led Spanish explorers to set sail for these lands, including Mexico, in search of gold. A group of Spanish explorers led by a nobleman named Hernán Cortés arrived in Mexico in 1519. They also wanted to convert the Maya to Christianity and colonize the area for Spain. The Spanish began to take control of the Yucatán by 1528, which led to the most widespread decline of the Maya living there. Mexico became a Spanish colony in 1535, but it was not until 1542, when their capital was established at Mérida, that the ancient Maya civilization was considered to have fallen. However, it was not until 1697 that Tayasal, the last independent Maya city-state, was conquered. By that time, the Spaniards had brought disease to the Maya and turned many Maya into slaves.

http://www.mariner.org/age/images/lg_palos.jpg - Microsoft Internet Explorer

File   Edit   View   Favorites   Tools   Help

Address http://www.mariner.org/age/images/lg_palos.jpg

Done   Internet

▲ *Christopher Columbus's landing in the Americas and the subsequent Spanish conquest of Mexico and Central America forever changed the history of the indigenous people of the region, including the Maya.*

▶ The Descendants of the Maya

Although the great ancient Maya civilization ended with the Spanish conquest of Mexico and Central America, there are today about 6 million descendants of the ancient Maya living throughout the region. These Maya speak any one of twenty-eight or more Mayan languages. The Yucatecs, the Tzotzil, and the Tzeltal live in Mexico. The Yucatecs live on the Yucatán Peninsula, while the Tzotzil and Tzeltal live in the highlands of Chiapas. The Quiche and Cakchiquel live in Guatemala. The Kekchí Maya live in Belize and Guatemala.

While many Maya today are Christians, they tend to interweave Christianity with ancient Maya ceremonial customs and beliefs. Local healers, priests, and shamans still provide the community with bodily and spiritual medicine. Agricultural ceremonies for the community are led by an *h-men* (which means "performer" or "doer"). It is his job to keep track of the round of days according to the Maya calendar. He also devises cures for the sick. A shaman deals more with matters of the spirit and ceremonial customs.[1]

Problems of the Modern-Day Maya

Many of today's Maya are farmers who, like their ancestors, plant and harvest corn, beans, and squash. Their children help their parents work the land, just as their ancestors did. But living conditions for most Maya today are often quite poor. Many times, entire families live in homes with a single room and little or no electricity or running water.

Guatemala's Petén region contains the largest expanse of rain forest left in Central America, but the Maya there have cleared much of it to grow corn. The population in this region has also increased from 15,000 in 1950 to more than 300,000 today, which has put an enormous strain on the area's natural resources.[2]

The Maya in Guatemala have faced discrimination since the time of the Spanish Conquest. In 1954, the elected government of Guatemala was overthrown by a military coup. The government had started to redistribute land from the wealthier "ladinos" (the mixed Spanish-Maya landowners) to the native Maya population. From 1954 until 1996, guerrilla armies fought against the military government. Traditional Maya were caught up in this

war when the guerrilla fighters demanded food and aid from them. The military also used civilian patrols to attack Maya villages suspected of harboring guerrilla fighters. The army and death squads are considered the main groups responsible for the nearly two hundred thousand Maya villagers killed during this period.

The 1992 Nobel Peace Prize was awarded to Rigoberta Menchú Tum, a Maya woman from Guatemala, for her work toward social justice for the indigenous people. She was interviewed in 1992, the year that marked the five-hundredth anniversary of Christopher Columbus's arrival in the Americas. When asked what she would do to mark the anniversary, she replied, "The struggle of the indigenous

▲ *Although the great ancient civilization of the Maya no longer exists, the descendants of the Maya do, in Mexico and in Central America.*

▲ *The Temple of Kukulcán at Chichén Itzá is also known as El Castillo,*
or the Castle. Great plumed serpent sculptures run down the sides of
the northern staircase.

did not begin in 1992, and it will not end in 1992; it is
simply an occasion to take advantage of the international
attention. . . . We are not myths of the past, ruins in the
jungle, or zoos. We are people and we want to be respected,
not to be victims of intolerance and racism."[3]

In 1996, a peace agreement was signed between the
Guatemalan government and the antigovernment fighters, and it included provisions for aid programs to help
the Maya. But troubles for the Maya continue elsewhere,
especially in the state of Chiapas in Mexico. In both
Guatemala and Mexico, violence against Maya people and
poverty within their communities remain serious prob-
lems, but there is some optimism that these people, the
descendants of a once-great civilization, will finally be
treated with the dignity and respect they deserve.

Chapter Notes

Chapter 1. The Mystery of the Ancient Maya

1. Victor Wolfgang Von Hagen, *Maya Explorer: John Lloyd Stephens and the Lost Cities of Central America and the Yucatán* (San Francisco: Chionicle Books, 1990), p. 215.

2. Stefan Lovgren, "Droughts Ended Maya Civilization, Experts Say," *National Geographic News*, March 13, 2003, <http://news.nationalgeographic.com/news/2003/03/0313_0303 13_mayadrought.html> (February 10, 2004).

Chapter 3. The Culture of the Ancient Maya

1. Robert J. Sharer, *The Ancient Maya* (Stanford: University Press, 1994), p. 482.

Chapter 5. The Ancient Maya Government

1. Simon Martin and Nikolai Grube, *Chronicle of the Maya Kings and Queens* (London: Thames & Hudson, Ltd., 2000), p. 17.

2. K. V. Flannery, ed., *The Cloud People: Divergent Evolution of the Zapotec and Mixtec Civilizations* (New York: Academic Press, 2003), pp. 79–80.

3. Robert J. Sharer, *The Ancient Maya* (Stanford: University Press, 1994), p. 493.

Chapter 6. The History of the Ancient Maya

1. Victoria Schlesinger, *Animals and Plants of the Ancient Maya* (Austin: University of Texas Press, 2001), p. 48.

2. *Canadian Museum of Civilization*, "Maya Civilization," n.d., <http://www.civilization.ca/civil/maya/mmc08eng.html> (January 5, 2004).

3. *Race and Ethnicity*, "Five Hundred Years of Sacrifice Before the Alien Gods," An Interview with Rigoberta Menchú Tum, n.d. <http://eserver.org/race/rigoberta-menchu-tum.html> (January 2, 2004).

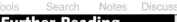
Further Reading

Braman, Arlette N. *The Maya: Activities and Crafts from a Mysterious Land.* Hoboken, N.J.: John Wiley & Sons, Inc., 2003.

Coe, Michael D. *The Maya.* New York: Thames and Hudson, 1999.

Coulter, Laurie. *Secrets in Stone: All About Maya Hieroglyphs.* Boston: Little, Brown Co., 2001.

Fisher, Leonard Everett. *Gods and Goddesses of the Ancient Maya.* New York: Holiday House, 1999.

Flood, Colleen Madonna. *The People of Mexico.* Philadelphia: Mason Crest Publishers, 2003.

Gerlach, Nancy, and Jeffrey Gerlach. *Foods of the Maya: A Taste of the Yucatán.* Albuquerque: University of New Mexico Press, 2002.

Lieurance, Suzanne. *Mexico: A MyReportLinks.com Book.* Berkeley Heights, N.J.: Enslow Publishers, Inc., 2004.

Lourie, Peter. *The Mystery of the Maya: Uncovering the Lost City of Palenque.* Honesdale, Pa.: Boyds Mill Press, 2001.

Macdonald, Fiona. *Find Out About the Aztecs and Mayas.* New York: Anness Publishing, Inc., 2001.

Mann, Elizabeth. *Tikal: The Center of the Maya World.* New York: Mikaya Press, 2002.

Netzley, Patricia D. *Maya Civilization.* San Diego, Calif.: Lucent Books, 2002.

Schlesinger, Arthur M., Jr. *Ancient Civilizations of the Aztecs and Maya.* Philadelphia: Chelsea House Publishers, 1999.

Schuman, Michael A. *Mayan and Aztec Mythology.* Berkeley Heights, N.J.: Enslow Publishers, Inc., 2001.

Sharer, Robert J. *Daily Life in Maya Civilization.* Westport, Conn.: Greenwood Press, 1996.

Shuter, Jane. *The Maya.* Chicago: Heinemann Library, 2002.